*Writer's Toolbox*

# WORLD INTEGRATION

## Other Works by Camille Picott
www.camillepicott.com

Indie Publishing Essentials: 9 Tools Every Author Needs
For Indie Success (Writer's Toolbox)

Creating Tension: Make Your Speculative Fiction Novel
A Page-Turner (Writer's Toolbox)

Sulan, Episode 1: The League

Sulan, Episode 1.5: Risk Alleviator

The Warrior & The Flower, 3 Kingdoms, Book 1

Raggedy Chan: A Chinese Heritage Tale, Book 1

Nine-Tail Fox: A Chinese Heritage Tale, Book 2

Raggedy Chan – the Illustrated Edition

*Writer's Toolbox*

# WORLD INTEGRATION

*How to Weave Worldbuilding into Your Speculative Fiction Novel*

By Camille Picott

Pixiu Press • Healdsburg, CA

www.camillepicott.com
camillepicott@gmail.com

ISBN 13: 978-1495470370
ISBN 10: 1495470377

Cover by Joey Manfre
www.joeyink.com

Copy Edit by Dani Crabtree
www.hedanicreations.net

For all who love other worlds

# CONTENTS

# Introduction to World Integration

## *How to Weave Worldbuilding into Your Speculative Fiction Novel*

Worldbuilding is the cornerstone of all good science fiction and fantasy. Readers love to be transported to other worlds and realities. There is no successful genre story without good worldbuilding.

What is worldbuilding? For those new to the genre, worldbuilding is the process of assembling all the minute details of a fictional world. These details include information on how culture, society, politics, magic, and/or science work in the fictional world where a story takes place. It also encompasses architecture, clothing, food, language, and even character back stories.

Once a writer has taken the time to create world details, the next task is determining how to incorporate this information into a story. This can present an interesting dilemma for genre writers. How can information on a fictional world be delivered to readers in a way that is natural to the story line? How can important details be shared without bogging down readers in pages and pages of boring exposition? (Also known as the dreaded "info dump".)

A delicate balance needs to be established. The reader needs enough information to maneuver in a novel's world, yet that information needs to be delivered in a way that doesn't smother the characters and plot.

This is where *World Integration* will help you. This book reveals writing techniques for incorporating worldbuilding into a novel. It will not discuss *how* to worldbuild. Rather, it will show specific methods for weaving worldbuilding details into genre fiction and discuss the pros and cons of each technique. Each method will be illustrated with examples from published novels. Some of the chosen books utilize more than one technique to show how methods can be mixed and matched for maximum effect.

By the end of the book, writers will have a toolbox full of writing techniques to enhance worldbuilding in their novels, as well as information to help assess which tools are best for their style of story.

*Writer's Toolbox*

# WORLD INTEGRATION

*How to Weave Worldbuilding into Your Speculative Fiction Novel*

# Pinches and Dashes

Have you ever heard people talk about adding a pinch of salt or a dash of pepper while cooking? This is also a world integration technique. Details are sprinkled in dialogue, character reactions, narration, and interior dialogue. Before you know it, these pinches and dashes of detail make the world come alive. This technique lends itself to seamless worldbuilding. It's what you'll see most frequently in science fiction and fantasy novels.

*Where this technique works*

This technique works effectively in stories with established tropes and/or familiar settings, such as urban and paranormal fantasies. Because authors use everyday settings and tropes familiar to readers—such as vampires, werewolves, faeries, and zombies—extensive details are not necessary. Readers already know vampires need blood to survive and werewolves turn into wolves. Readers also understand the basic workings of the setting. All authors need to do is flesh out minor details of their particular world.

*The Faerie Guardian* by Rachel Morgan is an example of this. Part of her novel takes place in a modern setting; the other part takes place in an alternative fae realm. The modern setting requires no explanation. Existing fae lore is incorporated into the novel, making extensive details on the fae realm unnecessary. The author does have some fun twists that she's added to her fae world, but all of these are seamlessly revealed with dialogue, character reactions, short narration, and interior monologues. In this excerpt, the faerie Violet has just rescued a human boy and is in the process of making a hasty exit:

I slide my hand into the top of my boot and retrieve my stylus. "You need to wake up and carry on studying," I tell the boy. Then I turn to the wall and scribble a few words across it. The writing glows and fades, and a portion of the wall melts away like ribbon held too close to a flame. "Goodbye," I call over my shoulder. I step into the yawning darkness, holding two words in my mind: Creepy Hollow.

With this short little snippet, readers learn exactly

how the faeries travel. The world integration is accomplished in a few short, concise sentences woven between dialogue. The reader gets information without ever losing the thread of the story.

Here's another example in *My Life As A White Trash Zombie* by Diana Rowland, also an urban fantasy. Zombie lore is well-known. The paranormal aspect of this novel doesn't require too much explanation. Rowland does give her zombies some special abilities, which she reveals throughout the story. In this excerpt, Angel, a new zombie, consumes brains after slamming her hand in the trunk of a car:

> I stopped dead, staring down at my left hand.
>
> The fingers were straight again. I slowly flexed them. No pain, not even a hint of it. The bones were most certainly in the right number of pieces. There was no swelling or blood—not even the slightest hint of a scrape.
>
> Oh my god.
>
> I swallowed hard then forced my legs to carry me back to my car. I hadn't imagined or hallucinated my hand getting slammed in the trunk. When I got back to my car I could definitely see flecks of blood on the edge of the trunk lid where my hand had been.
>
> The brains . . . they healed me up.

The power of brains—revealed in one short sentence—is woven into a fun scene complete with blood and broken body parts. It happens so quickly, readers barely have time to register the fact they've been hit with some world integration.

Both of these novels are full of many Pinches and Dashes examples.

## *Pitfalls*

While this technique is easiest to employ in stories utilizing tropes and familiar settings, it can be used for other genre books. As I said before, it is the most popular world integration technique. Just keep in mind that Pinches and Dashes can present challenges to writers tackling complex worlds. It can take authors in two dangerous directions:

*Info dump:* For those of you not familiar with this term, info dumping is a big no-no with science fiction and fantasy writers. Ever run across a long exposition chock-full of worldbuilding that's totally boring to read? That's an info dump. As writers tackle intricate worlds and try to weave information into their story, they can often end up divulging too much information. One paragraph will turn into ten, and before you know it, the reader is drowning in boring narration and impatiently waiting for the story to continue.

*Not enough information:* This is the opposite of info dumping. In trying to use the Pinches and Dashes technique, there's the risk of giving just enough information to leave readers confused. Since the whole point is to deliver details in quick sound bites, writers attempting to avoid info dumping may err on the side of being too spare with details.

I did just this in early drafts of my fantasy novel, *The Warrior & The Flower*. I sprinkled in lots of little details about a kylin (fantasy animal) over several chapters. Each time I did, my critique partners were left confused and wanting more details about the creature. They didn't get a full picture of the animal until three chapters in, and by that time, they were exasperated. I realized I needed to include all information on the animal in the first chapter, even if it meant treading dangerously close to info dumping.

With Pinches and Dashes, it's all about balance. Fans of the genre will forgive a story with a complex world if they understand it; they'll get cranky if they're confused or over saturated.

This technique is used successfully in *All These Things I've Done* by Gabrielle Zevin, a young adult dystopian novel. The setting is complex and cannot be revealed as easily as Morgan's fae world or Rowland's zombie world. Still, Zevin does an effective job of delivering bigger snippets of information while keeping the story flowing at a good pace. The novel opens with sixteen-year-old Anya describing her boyfriend's attempted date rape:

Admittedly, my taste in boys wasn't great. I was attracted to the sort who weren't in the habit of asking permission to do anything. Boys like my father, I guess.

We'd just gotten back from the coffee speakeasy that used to be off University Place, in the basement of a church. This was back when caffeine, along with about a million other things, was against the law. So much was illegal (paper without a permit, phones with cameras, chocolate, etc.) and the laws changed so quickly, you could be committing a crime and not even know it. Not that it mattered. The boys in blue were totally overwhelmed. The city was bankrupt, and I'd say maybe 75 percent of the force had been fired. The police that were left didn't have time to worry about teens getting high on coffee.

I should have known something was up when Gable offered to escort me back to the apartment.

While building up to Anya's confrontation with her boyfriend, Zevin weaves in narration that gives readers a snapshot of her dystopic setting. Her narrations are longer than those found in the other examples, but this is necessitated by the complexity of her world. Had Zevin chosen to cut back on her world integration, readers would not have enjoyed the full richness of her dystopian society.

The best you can do is to analyze your story carefully and make sure readers get enough information so they have a firm grasp of the world, but not so much that they're bored. Remember that this technique isn't the best for every novel. For techniques that are better suited to genre novels with intricate worlds, keep reading.

# Tell Me About It

This is a simple and effective way to integrate worldbuilding. It consists of one or more characters receiving important world and plot information from someone or something else. The readers gain insight as the characters gain insight. This technique gives writers the ability to share important information in a way that is natural to the plot.

## *Where this technique works*

*Conversation:* This is dialogue that takes place between two or more characters. One character asks questions (i.e., Do vampires really exist? How do you kill them?) and the other character answers them.

This is particularly effective when one character or group of characters is being introduced to a new world or society. The newcomers learn all about the rules and workings of the world from characters who are already part of it. The question-and-answer dialogue can be woven in seamlessly without feeling forced. This technique is common in urban fantasy, though it can be used in any genre novel.

This technique does not work well if all the characters are already "in the know" regarding the world you have created. Any dialogue about the workings of the world will seem forced and unnecessary if the characters are already fully submerged in it.

For an example of this, check out *Dirty Blood* by Heather Hildenbrand. Tara, a "normal" teenage girl, discovers she is from an ancient bloodline of werewolf hunters. As she is thrust into the world of the paranormal, those who take her in teach her its secrets. Here she talks with an adult werewolf and learns about the dangers of a werewolf bite:

"Werewolves have venom?"

Fee nodded again and her expression turned serious. "Don't forget that. It's the most important part. A Werewolf's bite is like poison to a Hunter. One bite, if left untreated, can kill you in the span of just a few hours."

"What about their nails?" I asked, remembering the scratches hidden under my shirt.

Fee shook her head. "They'll burn like crazy at the time, and you'll feel sore, but they'll heal on their own. The poison is in their saliva, which is why bites are dangerous."

If this conversation took place between two werewolves, it would not have been realistic since the characters would already know this information. It works well because the new hunter is being educated by an adult werewolf.

*Media:* This is an interaction between a character and a reference material: book, news recording, Internet, cyberspace, artificial intelligence, etcetera. The character that needs information obtains it through some form of media.

This technique can be used in any genre fiction that has the technology to share information—worlds that have virtual reality, television, newspaper, Internet, or radio. It can even work in fantasy worlds that have a type of magical device that can reach large groups of people, such as *The Daily Prophet* newspaper in the Harry Potter books.

You can see this technique in *Snow Crash* by Neil Stephenson. Hiro Protagonist journeys into cyberspace to investigate a new virus that's taking down hackers. He conducts much of his research with the Librarian, an interactive cyberspace software that "can move through the nearly infinite stacks of information in the Library with the agility of a spider dancing across a vast web of cross-references." In this excerpt, Hiro has the Librarian research specific information for him:

"Okay. Let's get some work done. Look up every piece of free information in the Library that contains L. Bob Rife and arrange it in chronological order. The emphasis here is on *free.*"

"Television and newspapers, yes, sir. One moment, sir," the Librarian says. He turns around and exits on crepe soles.

In the sections that follow, the Librarian retrieves vast amounts of information to share with Hiro—and the reader.

*Campfire Story:* This is when characters gain information from a song, poem, or oral story. Scenes like this will often take place in a setting where people gather, like a bar, party, tavern, or campfire. The technique works best in conveying important histories, myths, and legends of a society.

Many characters already know the histories and legends of their fictional world. Using a song or some other storytelling method allows writers the opportunity to share the stories without it seeming forced or unnatural.

Check out *The Name of the Wind* by Patrick Rothfuss to see this technique in action. Kvothe is a child born to a traveling troupe. He grows up performing at village festivals. Much of the important mythologies of this world are shared through the poems, stories, and plays of Kvothe's world. In this excerpt, Skarpi, an old man, shares stories with children at a dockside tavern.

"So, Lanre and the Creation War. An old, old story." His [Skarpi's] eyes swept over the children. "Sit and listen for I will speak of the shining city as it once was, years and miles away . . ."

Once, years and miles away, there was Myr Tariniel. The shining city. It sat among the tall mountains of the world like a gem on the crown of a king.

Readers hear an important mythological tale—a mythology that later plays a significant role in Kvothe's life.

## Pitfalls

Although Tell Me About It gives writers many different ways to reveal important worldbuilding details, it does have to be used with a sense of balance. There can be a tendency for Tell Me About It scenes to go on too long. You want to share just enough information to entertain and inform the reader, but not so much that they get bored or distracted from the main story thread. Monitor the length of your Tell Me About It scenes and make sure they don't get too lengthy.

# Direct Quotations

With this technique, *readers* (not characters) obtain direct quotes and excerpts from a written source—a newspaper, magazine, book, ancient scroll, etcetera. The written source can be completely fictional and should share important insight into the world. These quotations are often shared at the beginning of the novel, or at the beginning of each chapter. The idea is to present specific and "formal" details about the world in a succinct fashion that won't distract from the main narrative.

Remember that Direct Quotations are given straight to the reader. Unlike Tell Me About It, information is not received through a character's eyes.

## *Where this technique works*

This technique can be used in any genre fiction that has written communication. It can be especially helpful with complex worlds, as it gives authors a convenient way to world integrate. Writers can deliver world details in a way that doesn't distract from the flow of the main narrative.

Quotes can vary in length. For longer works, such as excerpts from a book or newspaper, consider presenting them at the beginning of the novel as a prologue or forward.

A good example can be found in *Eon* by Alison Goodman. Goodman presents an excerpt "From the Primer Scrolls of Jion Tzu," which helps readers learn about Dragoneyes, their role in society, the steep price they pay for their power, and about the dragons themselves:

Every New Year's Day the cycle turns, the next animal year begins, and its dragon becomes ascendant, his power doubling for that twelve months. The ascending dragon also unites with a new apprentice to be trained in the dragon magic, and as this boy steps up to his new life, the prior apprentice is promoted to Dragoneye and into his full power. He replaces his master, the old Dragoneye, who retires exhausted and fatally debilitated by his twenty-four-year union with the dragon. It is a brutal bargain that gives a Dragoneye enormous power—enough to move monsoons, redirect rivers, and stop earthshakes.

Shorter quotes can be presented at the beginning of every chapter. Examples of this can be found in *Nice Girls Don't Have Fangs* by Molly Harper. Many quotes are from *The Guide for the Newly Undead, a* made-up non-fiction work that exists in this paranormal world. Each of these quotes contains important information about vampirism. The quotes are both entertaining and informative. Here are some examples:

While it's tempting to try and resume your normal social activities with still-living friends, you must understand that some people will have difficulty adjusting to your new condition. Warning signs that loved ones may be planning to stake you include a sudden interest in carpentry and staring at your chest to gauge where your heart is located. —From *The Guide for the Newly Undead*

Remember, you're much more flammable now than you were in life. So live every day as if you're soaked in gasoline. —From *The Guide for the Newly Undead*

Brandon Sanderson's epic fantasy Mistborn series also has quotes at the beginning of each chapter. In this example from *Hero of Ages* (the third book in the series), readers learn about Allomancy:

Snapping has always been the dark side of Allomancy. A person's genetic endowment may make them a potential

Allomancer, but in order for the power to manifest, the body must be put through extraordinary trauma.

## *Pitfalls*

The caution with this technique is to make sure you don't go overboard with long excerpts. A ten-page discourse on the history of sorcery will probably bore your reader, while a one or two page excerpt could prove an interesting and fun read.

# Sightseeing

Sightseeing is a technique where details are revealed as a character physically moves through a setting. The setting can be a town, castle, countryside, spaceship—anything. The character can be walking, flying in a zephyr, riding a horse, etcetera. As characters encounter details of the setting, their observations are shared with the reader. These details boost the worldbuilding. It's not just the physical setting that can be revealed, but also details of culture, architecture, and political undercurrents.

*Where this technique works*

In just about any book, characters at some point have to get from point A to point B. As long as characters have a realistic reason to make their trek, this technique can be used.

A book that does this is *The Demon Trapper's Daughter* by Jana Oliver. In the beginning of this dystopian novel, Riley makes a car trip from one end of Atlanta to the other. Details of the setting are woven seamlessly into the narrative as she heads toward her destination.

> The biggest problem was the empty air above the intersection: the traffic lights were gone.
>
> "They keep this up and there won't be one damned light left in this city," Beck complained.
>
> Most of them had been stolen for scrap by metal thieves. It took some guts to climb up on those things in the middle of the night and dismantle them. Every now and then a thief slipped and ended up a grease spot on the road, buried in a tangle of metal.

By the time Riley reaches her destination, readers have learned a lot about her world. The city is bankrupt and cannot afford to replace the stolen traffic lights, making the roads hazardous. Food is hard to come by, and there are long lines in front of soup kitchens. Readers even meet reanimated corpses purchased by rich people as servants.

Another example of this technique can be found in *Across the Nightingale Floor* by Lian Hearn. As Kaede travels through the country to meet her betrothed, readers gain visual and cultural details:

They traveled until midday, rested for a while at an inn, and then went on for another few miles before evening. By the time they stopped, Kaede's mind was reeling with all she had seen: the brilliant green of the rice fields, as smooth and luxuriant as the pelt of an animal; the white splashing rivers that raced beside the road; the mountains that rose before them, range after range, clad in their rich summer green, interwoven with the crimson of wild azaleas. And the people on the road, of every sort and description: warriors in armor, bearing swords and riding spirited horses; farmers carrying all manner of things that she'd never seen before; oxcarts and packhorses, beggars and peddlers.

She was not supposed to stare at them, and they were supposed to bow low to the ground as the procession went past, but she sneaked as many looks at them as they did at her.

Not only do readers get to "see" the gorgeous Japanese-inspired landscape and the people who live there, but they also gain an understanding of how royalty is treated.

## Pitfalls

If using this technique, try to weave in the details of the world as seamlessly as possible into the scene. Be careful of bogging down the pace of your story with too much information. The trick is to deliver enough details to interest the reader and set the stage of your world without stalling the story.

# Culinary Detail

Culinary Detail is a technique that allows writers to integrate world information with food descriptions. Every region in the world has something special that it offers in terms of local cuisine. If your story is set in the south, maybe your character likes grits and sweet tea. If your story takes place in Napa, California, there's probably going to be wine involved. Characters in outer space might have nothing but protein sludge, or perhaps receive their food intravenously.

Food can also reveal details about your character. Maybe you have a character on the Paleo Diet or the Atkins Diet. Maybe you have a character who is allergic to shellfish or gluten, or maybe you have a character who is a raw foodist. You can do so many fun things with food, all of which enhance your reader's overall worldbuilding experience.

## *Where this technique works*

You can have a lot of fun with this in a fantasy or sci-fi setting, but even mundane settings can benefit from Culinary Detail. And there is always something to be learned about what and how a character eats.

One of the best examples of this technique can be found in Cindy Pon's *Silver Phoenix*. It's a fantasy novel that takes place in an Asian setting. Here's an excerpt from Pon's detail-rich novel, where three travel companions share a meal after a long journey:

"There's hot goat's milk for your morning meal, along with sticky rice balls with sweetened taro, rice porridge with pickled vegetables and salted pork, and the most amazing fruit you've ever tasted." Li Rong waved his arm in a flourish toward a lacquered tray laden with food at the end of her bed.

"We couldn't wait for you," Chen Yong said, although he didn't sound apologetic. She didn't mind. She wouldn't have waited either.

She scooted to the end of the bed and picked up a sticky rice ball and bit into it. Sweet things first. The chewy taro paste within had just the right hint of sugar. "Mmm," she managed with her mouth full.

Not only do the food descriptions enhance the Asian setting, but we also learn that this heroine likes her sweets, which helps readers understand her zestful nature. There are lots of nice details woven into the narrative that add dimension to setting and character.

In *My Life As A White Trash Zombie* by Diana Rowland, there are also examples of Culinary Detail. In this excerpt, several friends sit down together in a restaurant:

I waved toward the empty chairs around the table. "Y'all wanna sit? I'm killing some time."

In answer, both men seized chairs and sat. The waitress materialized and slid my pie in front of me, then turned to Ed and Marcus. "Y'all eatin'?"

Ed smiled. "Yes, ma'am. I'll have the double bacon cheeseburger with fries, loaded baked potato, cinnamon apples, mac and cheese, and a side salad with ranch dressing. Oh, and a Barq's."

"And I'll have a Diet Coke," Marcus said as soon as the waitress had finished scrawling down Ed's incredible order. "Also a turkey club with extra bacon, a cup of gumbo, garlic bread, and an Italian salad—with extra olive oil."

Some of the foods ordered by these characters, such as cinnamon apples and gumbo, are common in the American South, where this story takes place. Readers get some nice regional detail. We also learn that two of these main characters have tremendous appetites.

## Pitfalls

Be careful not to get overzealous with food descriptions. Your readers don't want to read ten pages devoted to describing a breakfast. (I'm exaggerating here, but you get the point.) Otherwise, have fun with this technique and let it work to your advantage.

# What to Wear

Details about the clothing and accessories worn by characters can do a lot to enhance a fictional world. The What to Wear technique includes anything worn on the body of a character—jewelry, weapons, makeup, hairstyle, and even tattoos. If characters show up dressed from head to toe in furs, readers can bet they are 1) not from a tropical locale, and 2) not members of PEETA. If a samurai shows up with a rifle slung over one shoulder, readers know they are in for some genre bending. You can have a lot of fun with What to Wear and really use it to amplify the world.

*Where this technique works*

Clothing detail works best when used to highlight the unique qualities of a fictional world. Steer away from mundane descriptions of jeans and T-shirts when you can. Focus on clothing aspects that highlight what's different about your world. We write science fiction and fantasy, which always leaves room for something unique on the body.

In this excerpt from *City of Bones* by Cassandra Clare, we get a glimpse of some unique ink markings on a teenage girl in a nightclub:

> There was some sort of bracelet around her wrist, just under the cuff of her dress—then, as he neared her, he saw that it wasn't a bracelet at all but a pattern inked into her skin, a matrix of swirling lines.
>
> He froze.

The ink patterns on her skin turn out to be runes, a powerful form of magic used by the characters in this novel. This is the reader's first glimpse of the supernatural element in this novel.

Here is a description of the clothing worn by the wife of a samurai in *Daughter of the Sword* by Steve Bien:

> Hisami was a beautiful woman, statuesque, not tiny and frail like the courtesans so many women tried to imitate. Of course Saito was long-boned himself, and so Hisami stood only to his shoulder. Among the other ladies, however, she held herself proud and tall like a hunting falcon on the wrist, sleek neck and gleaming eyes, knowing no fear. Today her kimono was pale orange with her

underrobe showing the purest white. Her hair was, as ever, immaculate, wide set with two long pins retaining her bun. Saito knew for a fact what anyone else might have guessed: that the pins were actually knives. For Hisami was samurai like her husband, and equally prepared to take up arms and spill her life's blood at her master's command.

The hairpins are a lovely detail, showing the strict loyalty and obedience expected of samurai culture. Not only can Hisami fight, but she is also willing to commit *seppuku* if so ordered—the Japanese ritual suicide by disembowelment.

*Stormdancer* by Jay Kristoff is a Japanese steampunk. This unique setting is captured in the clothing worn by the heroine Yukiko:

She wore an outfit of sturdy gray cloth, unadorned save for a small fox embroidered on the breast, cut simply for the sake of utility. An uwagi tunic covered her from neck to mid-thigh, open at the throat, long, loose sleeves with folded cuffs rippling in the feeble breeze. An obi sash of black silk was wrapped tight around her waist, six inches wide, tied in a simple bow at the small of her back. A billowing pair of hakama trousers trailed down to her feet, which were covered by a pair of split-toed tabi socks. Long hair flowed around her shoulders, midnight black against pale, smooth skin. A gray kerchief was tied over her mouth, polarized glass lenses trimmed with thin brass and black rubber covering her eyes.

This description of Yukiko perfectly reveals the

blend of Japanese influence and steampunk in this novel. The uwagi tunic, obi sash, and split-toed tabi socks are combined with the brass-and-rubber polarized lenses she wears to protect her eyes from pollution.

## *Pitfalls*

It can be a lot of fun to delve into the minute details of clothing. A word of warning: if you find yourself getting long-winded about the types of beads on a headdress, make sure you've got the right audience for it. This works in epic fantasy novels, where fans expect heavy tomes chock-full of details. However, heavy description slows down the pace of a story, so it might not be as appropriate for a fast-paced urban fantasy or a high-octane space opera.

# Authentic Language

Worldbuilding isn't just about finessing a futuristic science or perfecting a magic system, but also about how characters speak in these worlds. The language of your characters can make a significant contribution to your world integration. Authentic Language can be woven into dialogue and narration. Language can be used to convey culture, upbringing, time period, and character background.

*Where this technique works*

This technique can be used in any type of genre fiction. As you write, consider how the words of your character can enhance the details of a world.

One of my favorite television shows is *Firefly*, a sci-fi western by Joss Whedon. His characters speak a mixture of "Wild-Wild West" English and Chinese. It reveals just how cultures have melded in this futuristic world.

*The Dead of Winter* by Lee Collins is an urban fantasy set in the Old West. In this excerpt, you can see how the texture of his world is conveyed in the language of the characters:

> "What's wrong, sir?" Jack asked.
>
> "Something ain't right here," the marshal said, not looking up. "We got us a pair of wolfers killed by something violent, but their dogs got away clean." He pointed to a set of tracks leading away from the clearing. "See there? Them dogs wasn't even bloody when they lit out, meaning they wasn't in a fight at all. They just upped and ran, letting the poor fools with them get torn to bits."
>
> "Can't say I blame them," Jack said. "Whatever killed them fellers did it right quick, and was awful messy about it."

After reading this exchange, most readers would not even need to be told the story takes place in the Old West; it's inferred by the language.

*Peacemaker* by Lindsay Buroker is a steampunk novella set in the Yukon during the gold rush. Buroker uses language to transport her reader to her particular setting:

> "You ought to let the girl go back to her kin, Cedar," Jane said, and Cedar lifted his gaze from the talisman for the first time since they had sat down. "It ain't right to risk her life just so you can get

your hammertoes warmed at night," Jane finished.

The word *hammertoes* originated in the late 1880s, which is the same time period of this story. It's a perfect way to reveal time period to readers. Even if readers aren't familiar with the origin of the word hammertoes, it's an unusual enough word to transport the reader to a different setting and culture.

## *Pitfalls*

There is sometimes a tendency, especially in high fantasy, to use a lot of made-up words, and in some cases, to create an entirely new language. Many Star Trek fans are fluent in Klingon. J.R.R. Tolkien created several languages for Middle-Earth.

It is good to remember that made-up words and languages require extra effort from readers. Like all forms of world integration, Authentic Language needs to be used with a sense of balance. Though Tolkien did create several languages for Middle-Earth, they are used sparingly. Here is a quote from Treebeard in *The Two Towers*:

"Hmm, did he now?" rumbled Treebeard. "And I might have said much the same, if you had been going the other way. Do not risk getting entangled in the woods of *Laurelindórenan*. That is what the Elves used to call it, but now they make the name shorter: Lothlórien they call it. Perhaps they are right: maybe it is fading;

not growing. Land of the Valley of Singing Gold, that was it, once upon a time. Now it is the Dreamflower. Ah well! But it is a queer place, and not for just any one to venture in. I am surprised that you ever got out, but much more surprised that you ever got in: that has not happened to strangers for many a year. It is a queer land.

"And so is this. Folk have come to grief here. Aye, they have, to grief. *Laurelindórenan lindelorendor malinornélion ornemalin*," he hummed to himself. "They are falling rather behind the world in there, I guess," he said. "Neither this country, nor anything else outside the Golden Wood, is what it was when Celeborn was young."

If the entire novel were written in elvish, it wouldn't have interested many readers. Instead, the authentic language is used just enough to give readers the sense of a vast, ancient world with many cultures, but not so much that readers need to keep an elvish dictionary on hand.

There is a point where a novel can become saturated with an invented language. It can become difficult and frustrating for readers to keep track of what every word means. A good rule of thumb is to use made-up words only for things that are unique to your world. For common things, stick with common terms. (If you're describing a mouse, just call it a mouse.) You are asking for extra effort on the part of your reader when you invent a language or new words. Make sure that effort enhances the world.

# Flashbacks

Flashbacks are stories relayed as memories within the main narrative of a novel. They can be both incredibly effective and incredibly risky to use. I once attended a writer's conference and was told that writers should never, *ever* use flashbacks. And while I agree there are some risks to be had, there are many novels where they are used effectively.

*Where this technique works*

*Shorts:* Flashbacks are easier to manage if they are kept short. The shorter they are, the less chance there is to lose or bore readers. A few sentences or short paragraphs inserted into the narrative can reveal a lot to readers without becoming the dreaded info-dump.

A book that does this well is *Daughter of the Sword*

by Steve Bein. The main character, Mariko, is a native-born Japanese who spent part of her childhood in the United States. Bein weaves in a number of short flashbacks to give readers insight into how Mariko's life was profoundly affected by her time spent in the States. She has a cultural perspective not common among her fellow Japanese police officers, which in turn gives readers insight into Japanese culture. None of the flashbacks is long and they do not interrupt the pace of the novel. In this excerpt, Mariko recalls the forced retirement of her former boss:

Not for the first time, she wished to hell Lieutenant Hashimoto hadn't retired. Not that he'd had much choice. Like Mariko, the man had no idea how to do anything halfway. Twenty-six years of eighty-hour workweeks had taken their toll, until finally he'd passed out in his office and woken up to a doctor telling him he was a near case of *karoshi*. *Karoshi*: death from overwork. What did it mean about Japanese culture that they had a word for that? How could a society survive where so many people worked themselves to death that they had no choice but to come up with a name for it? The Americans had no equivalent— but, then, the existence of the term *drive-by shooting* was every bit as biting a commentary on their culture. Only in a place of unremitting violence could people invent vocabulary to separate *this* kind of shooting each other from *that* kind of shooting each other.

In one concise paragraph, readers gain a deeper understanding of Japanese culture and Mariko's world.

More examples of short flashbacks can be found in *All These Things I've Done* by Gabrielle Zevin. Sixteen-year-old Anya wakes in the middle of the night to screams of her little sister. Anya rushes to her sister's side and shakes her awake from a nightmare. As Anya consoles her, she recalls the murder of their father in this short flashback:

> The killers came while Daddy was working. Not only had Natty and I been home, we'd been in the room with him. No one saw us because we'd been playing at Daddy's feet, concealed by the frame of his massive mahogany desk. He heard the intruders before he saw them. Daddy tilted his head toward us ever so slightly and put his finger to his lips. "Don't move" had been his last words, right before he was shot in the head. Even though I was still a child I knew enough to clamp my hand over Natty's mouth so that no one could hear her sobs. And though no one was there to clamp a hand over my own mouth, I didn't cry either.
>
> They shot Daddy once in the head and three times in the chest and then they ran out of the house. From my position under the desk, I didn't see who did it, and the police still consider the crime unsolved. Not that they investigated it very much. I mean, Daddy had been a notorious crime boss—from their point of view, his murder was only a matter of time, an occupational hazard, etcetera. On some level, maybe they even thought the murderers had done them a favor.

In two short paragraphs, readers learn poignant details of Anya's childhood and gain a better understanding of her world. We see that Anya lives in a world of crime and that, from a young age, has been the caretaker of her younger sister.

*Humorous:* While short and concise flashbacks are the safest route to go, there are instances where long flashbacks work quite well. Humorous recollections are a way to both entertain and inform your reader. Novels that use this technique have what many would consider heavy info dumping via flashbacks. However, these flashbacks are filled with so much rich detail and hilarity that it's impossible not to get sucked in and enjoy the backstory.

In *How to Seduce a Naked Werewolf* by Molly Harper, Mo (short for Moonflower), moves to Alaska in a desperate attempt to escape her overbearing, tree-hugging parents. The beginning of the novel is filled with many pages about Mo's childhood and her desperate attempt to find a "normal" life away from her parent's hippie commune. These stories are hilarious, entertaining, and give the readers lots of insight into the main character and the world she was raised in. If they weren't so funny, they would have been boring to read.

This excerpt shows Mo's campaign to break away from her hippie parents and go to public school:

That afternoon marked the first argument I'd had with my parents—well, with my mother. My father seemed to think that if my parents were going to encourage me to make my own choices, that should include supporting me when those choices included public school. My mother warned me of dire consequences, peer pressure, the influence of uncaring and underqualified teachers, a revisionist curriculum that would only prepare me for life as a drone, and, worse yet, refined sugars in the cafeteria food. But she eventually signed the enrollment papers, and I was the newest student in Leland High School's ninth grade.

This flashback goes on for quite a few pages, but from this snippet the reader gains a firm (and humorous) impression of the culture of Mo's childhood.

*Emotionally Charged:* Long flashbacks can also be effective when the scene is emotionally charged. Revealing a traumatic memory exposes readers to characters and their world.

An excellent emotionally charged flashback is Chapter 2 of *The Hunger Games* by Suzanne Collins. In the hardback edition, the flash back is six-and-a-half pages long. It reveals many things, including Katniss's grief over the death of her father, her mother's downward spiral into depression, and Katniss's days of starvation before she learned to hunt. And most importantly, it shows readers her first meeting with Peeta, her fellow tribute to the Hunger Games:

Suddenly a voice was screaming at me and I looked up to see the baker's wife, telling me to move on and did I want her to call the Peacekeepers and how sick she was of having those brats from the Seam pawing through her trash. The words were ugly and I had no defense. As I carefully replaced the lid and backed away, I noticed him, a boy with blond hair peering out from behind his mother's back. I'd seen him at school. He was in my year, but I didn't know his name. He stuck with the town kids, so how would I?

Not only do readers experience this first significant meeting between Katniss and Peeta, they also learn important world information, such as the class separation in Katniss's district and the difficulty lower-class residents have finding food. It is poignant and engrossing, and reveals much of Katniss's harsh dystopian reality.

Another example of a lengthy, emotionally charged flashback can be found in *Hero* by Perry Moore. In a twelve-page flashback, readers gain a deeper understanding of Thom's poor neighborhood and his relationship with his father. Most importantly, readers learn about the superheroes and super-villains of this world.

In this excerpt, cat burglars stumble across the medal cabinet of a former superhero, who happens to be Thom's father:

"Shit," another guy said from across the room. He'd found Dad's trophy case, his medals, all his commendations.

The moonlight reflected off an old medal the president had once given Dad for single-handedly fending off an invasion of telepathic starfish-shaped aliens and illuminated a very distinct impression on the thug's face. Panic.

Readers see that this is not a normal, everyday world; rather, it is a world plagued by exotic super-villains and protected by superheroes.

## *Pitfalls*

Like other forms of world integration, writers have to maintain a delicate balance with flashbacks. When using them, you run several risks: 1) pulling readers out of the story, 2) stalling the story and losing the interest of readers, and 3) slowing down the story's pace.

In all of these flashback examples, readers are temporarily taken out of the main story. The trade off is deeper characterization and better world integration. Consider if your flashback is important enough to warrant using. Always pay particular attention to the length of the flashback. The longer it is, the higher the risk of interrupting the main story.

# Fictional Memoir

This technique is an extension of the flashback, although unique enough that it deserves its own section. The Fictional Memoir is just that—a story told memoir-style with the narrator reflecting back on the significant periods of his life in chronological order.

*Where this technique works*

Fictional Memoir can be used in any genre novel. This technique helps authors handle large casts of characters, long periods of time (often decades), evolving political situations, and highly detailed backstories. It's a particularly useful tool for those who write epic novels.

The key with Fictional Memoir is the narrator's ability to reflect on past events and past time periods, something a character cannot do in a conventional narrative. These reflections have the advantage of imparting many valuable details to readers. In a memoir, reflections are expected. In conventional narrative, characters do not have the advantage of hindsight. There is no opportunity for reflection.

Many examples of Fictional Memoir can be found in *The Name of the Wind* by Patrick Rothfuss. Kvothe relates the story of his childhood to a scribe. The tale spans about a decade of his life, beginning with his childhood as a traveling performer, to his adolescence as a homeless street orphan, and to his late teen years as a successful university student and musician. In this excerpt, Kvothe reflects upon his time as an orphan in the city of Tarbean:

I had been in Tarbean for years at this point. Three birthdays had slipped by unnoticed and I was just past fifteen. I knew how to survive Waterside. I had become an accomplished beggar and thief. Locks and pockets opened to my touch. I knew which pawnshops bought goods "from uncle" with no questions asked.

I was still ragged and frequently hungry, but I was in no real danger of starving. I had been slowly building my rainy-day money. Even after a hard winter that had frequently forced me to pay for a warm spot to sleep, my hoard was over twenty iron pennies. It was like a dragon's treasure to me.

I had grown comfortable there. But aside from the desire to add to my rainy-day money I had nothing to live for. Nothing driving me. Nothing to look forward to. My days were spent looking for things to steal and ways to entertain myself.

As Kvothe recalls his childhood in this example, readers not only get character backstory, which is an important part of world integration, but they also get a snapshot of the city where the character lives: the seedier pawn shops, the hard winters, and the sad fate of homeless children.

Another novel with many examples of Fictional Memoir is *Kushiel's Dart* by Jacqueline Carey. This book covers about twenty years of the life of Phèdre. Throughout the tale, Phèdre delivers a lot of information through reflection. Such as: political happenings, religious history, and summaries of her childhood and adolescence. In this example, Phèdre discusses her mentor's techniques for selecting her consorts:

> I understood, later, why he held me back during those first long years. Those whom Delaunay would choose for his clientele would be chosen with care. They were among the elite and mistrustful of the nation, too deeply embroiled in money and power to be lured easily into spilling pillow-secrets.

Readers learn much about Phèdre's culture in this short paragraph. She moves in the dangerous society of the wealthy and powerful. In another excerpt from the same novel, readers gain an insight into a vast political web:

I learned that Gaspar Trevalion, Comte de Fourcay and kinsman to Marc, Duc de Trevalion, was a great friend of his. A clever, cynical man with streaks of gray at his temples, Gaspar was adept at snipping the political winds to see which way they blew. It was he, doubtless, who had told Delaunay how the Princess Lyonette whispered in her son Baudoin's ear about an ailing King and an empty throne, and the portent people might take from the symbolic wedding at the Midwinter Masque.

As you can see, Fictional Memoir is a useful tool for exposing aspects of worlds that are both important and intricate.

## *Pitfalls*

There are two risks when using a memoir-style.

*Distance:* It can create a distance between the reader and the action. The action in the story can become less immediate, which hinders the overall piece.

*Slow Pace:* It also produces a book that has slower pacing, so consider if this technique is right for your target audience. For example, this might not be the best technique if you're writing a young adult novel, which tends to be fast paced. The novels mentioned above— *Kushiel's Dart* and *The Name of the Wind*—are hefty tomes with moderate pacing, but this is acceptable among fans of epic fantasy.

While this technique can be an effective tool, analyze

your manuscript and make sure it's the best approach for your audience.

# Back In The Day

With this technique, a novel opens with an important event that happens "back in the day"–that is, long before the main story begins. The opening can take place years, decades, or even centuries prior to the novel's story. This is often used as a prologue or first chapter.

*Where this technique works*

This is a way to show readers the details of an important historical or mythological event that plays a significant role in the main plot of a story. It can be effective to "show" the important event as a scene, as opposed to "telling" readers about it through some other method. With an actual scene, there are opportunities to share details and complexities that otherwise would be difficult to communicate.

If you have a backstory or mythology that's too complex to relate with any other technique, this is one to consider. It's always good to "show" rather than "tell" when you have the opportunity.

The novel *Become* by Ali Cross uses this technique in a prologue. The story opens with a man named Elario helping the lover of Lucifer give birth to the devil's child in secret. The prologue ends with Lucifer tracking down his infant child and taking her back to hell:

He [Elario] blinked away the tears as his vision slipped— sometimes he saw the Dark One, a shadow of blackest night, his beating wings crashing through the low ceiling. And then as he blinked, as he tried to see the one he had fought against his entire existence, he thought he saw . . . a man.

Elario fell to his knees, looking to the child now cradled in his arms. She gazed at him, her gold-flecked eyes shining with determination and courage. She smiled.

"Dios . . ." But the prayer Elario might have uttered slipped from his lips as the man gently took his daughter and stepped into the abyss.

Chapter 1 then flashes forward many years as readers are introduced to Desolation, the teenage daughter of Lucifer:

If he weren't Father's right-hand man, Akaros would be dead. I clenched my fists, felt the nails bite my flesh. Akaros shook with laughter—but instead of retaliating, I pulled ragged, calming breaths through my burning throat.

"You're holding yourself back, Desolation." Akaros' voice boomed through the featureless training room.

Utilizing this technique allows Cross to show readers the unfortunate beginning of Desolation's life, where she is abducted by her father and taken to be raised in hell. This backstory packed a lot of punch when revealed as a scene in the prologue. If it had been revealed through another method—perhaps with Tell Me About It or Pinches and Dashes—readers would not have been able to witness and fully understand this important event that shaped the rest of Desolation's life.

## *Pitfalls*

There are two major risks to using this technique.

*Two Beginnings:* Novels using this method begin with a scene set many years outside the main story. This requires readers to "orientate" themselves to two beginnings—once to the backstory, then to the second, "real" opening of the novel. Since readers might not be able to immerse themselves in the story and world immediately, this technique can make it difficult to hook them right out of the gate.

*Leading with Minor Characters:* Since this type of opening takes place long before the main story begins, it is often necessary to populate with minor characters.

(Unless there are supernatural characters who live for hundreds of years, in most cases the main character isn't alive during these historical events.) A second drawback to this technique is that it can be difficult for readers to develop a connection to a character they may or may not see again in the course of a novel. This, too, can make it difficult to hook the reader right out of the gate.

Robert Jordan's *The Eye of The World* is a great example of Back In The Day, but it also illustrates the two pitfalls encountered with this technique. This epic fantasy begins with a prologue written from the point of view of Lews Therin Telamon, a powerful man who became known as the Kinslayer after he went mad and murdered his entire family:

> Lews Therin Telamon wandered the palace, deftly keeping his balance when the earth heaved. "Ilyena! My love, where are you?" The edge of his pale gray cloak trailed through blood as he stepped across the body of a woman, her golden-haired beauty marred by the horror of her last moments, her still-open eyes frozen in disbelief. "Where are you, my wife? Where is everyone hiding?"

Chapter 1 flashes forward to a new age and readers meet Rand al'Thor, the reincarnation of Lews Therin Telamon:

> Gusts plastered Rand al'Thor's cloak to his back, whipped the earth-colored wool around his legs, then streamed out behind him.

He wished his coat were heavier, or that he had worn an extra shirt.

This novel essentially has two beginnings: the prologue, where we meet the Kinslayer, and chapter one, where we meet the Kinslayer's reincarnation, the true protagonist. Just as readers begin to find their sea legs in the world of the Kinslayer, they are thrust into the time of Rand al'Thor.

They also do not meet the Kinslayer again in the novel. It's hard to care about a character that disappears from the story.

While this technique has its place, it comes with a set of risks. If you plan to use Back In The Day, step back and evaluate your novel to make sure it's the best choice.

# Story Within A Story

This technique is exactly as it states: a story within a story. Threaded within the main story is either one or several short stories. These shorts are self-contained stories with a beginning, middle, and end that take place outside of the main story. Their function is to reveal important backstory and enhance the depth and details of the main plot. They are used to reveal important historical and mythological aspects that otherwise would be too cumbersome to share with readers.

This technique is similar to Back In The Day, but there are two major differences: 1) the backstories are much longer and complex, and 2) the stories are woven throughout the novel, not necessarily presented at the beginning.

## Where this technique works

This technique can work well if your novel has a complex backstory or mythology that can't be revealed with any of the other techniques discussed in this book.

A book that uses this technique is *Daughter of the Sword* by Steve Bein. The main story of the novel takes place in modern-day Tokyo. A female detective finds herself investigating a murder case that involves three enchanted samurai swords: Beautiful Singer, Glorious Victory Unsought, and Tiger on the Mountain. Each of these swords has a unique enchantment.

Woven throughout the modern day detective story are three short stories, each of them revealing the secrets of the enchanted blades. The first short story takes place in the Kamakura Era of the samurai (1308 CE) and reveals the dangerous nature of Beautiful Singer. The next takes place in the Azuchi-Momoyama Era of the samurai (1587 CE) and explores the power and danger of Glorious Victory Unsought. And the last story takes place in the Showa Era of World War II (1942 CE) and shows the nature of Tiger on the Mountain. Without these detailed short stories, the power and danger of the blades would have been impossible to appreciate fully.

Another novel with a Story Within a Story is *Daughter of Smoke and Bone* by Laini Taylor. The bulk of the novel centers on the story of Karou, a teenage girl living in Prague, and Akiva, the tormented angel who loves her. A secret from Akiva's past has a profound impact on his relationship with Karou. Bits of Akiva's secret are hinted at throughout the novel, but they are not fully revealed until the last hundred pages of the book. These hundred pages are a separate story devoted entirely to Akiva's past, and take up roughly 25 percent of the entire novel. The depth of his love for Karou and his inner conflict would not be fully appreciated without this story within a story.

## Pitfalls

Readers either love or hate this technique. Those who love it appreciate the extra depth these stories within a story add to the overall world and plot. Those who hate it feel it detracts from the main story. They get impatient for the "real" story thread to continue.

It's ultimately a matter of choice. If you want to see if this technique is right for your novel, I suggest picking up one of the books discussed above. See if you're a reader who loves this technique, or hates it.

# Acknowledgments

Thanks to all my wonderful beta readers!

Arlene Ang
Lan Chan
Chris Picott
M.G. Alves, Jr.
Dinesh Pulandram

# About the Author

Camille Picott is an award-winning author of numerous science fiction and fantasy works. Several of her novels are Amazon Bestsellers, and she has published over a dozen shorts stories. *Writers Toolbox* was born from her blog column, *The Writer's View*. To learn more about Camille, visit www.camillepicott.com.